Do you want to be the sort of girl who is liked by everybody; who is showered with all kinds of jolly invitations; who has hosts of friends; who always has plenty of "dates" with attractive young men? In short, do you want to be popular?

Study this little book, and when you have mastered its contents, put them into practice. You will be rewarded by a feeling of poise and confidence, and the knowledge that you are popular with all with whom you come in contact - that you are what is known as "a social success."

HAWKE

SOCIAL SUCCESS
THE MODERN GIRL'S GUIDE

A BOOK OF ETIQUETTE
FOR ALL OCCASIONS

Copper Beech Publishing

Published in Great Britain by
Copper Beech Publishing Ltd

Editor Jan Barnes
Originally published as part of the 'Home Notes' series by
C.Arthur Pearson Ltd/IPC Media Ltd and reproduced
by kind permission.

ISBN
978 1 898617 37 2
1 898617 37 6
A CIP catalogue record for this book is available from The
British Library.

Copper Beech Gift Books
Copper Beech Publishing Ltd
PO Box 159 East Grinstead
Sussex England RH19 4FS
www.copperbeechpublishing.co.uk

INTRODUCTION

Do you want to be the sort of girl who is liked by everybody; who is showered with all kinds of jolly invitations; who has hosts of friends; who always has plenty of "dates" with attractive young men? In short, do you want to be popular?
The answer is in the affirmative, isn't it? It is only right and natural that it should be.

Now, the first step to popularity is
Good Manners
- which can be acquired by anyone with a little trouble and patience. But remember that good manners will not come easily and sit unobtrusively upon you (as they should) unless you have a kind heart and a sympathetic nature as a foundation upon which to build.

Another little virtue which is often overlooked by those in search of social success is -

Tact

This is a quality which smooths over difficulties, eases awkward situations, and generally makes life a much pleasanter affair.

To be tactful, you need a ready imagination. Put yourself in the other person's place, and you will find it perfectly easy to avoid saying or doing anything which may cause annoyance or embarrassment.

Then, to round off and perfect an attractive personality, you must acquire easy, graceful manners, springing from a thorough knowledge of all the usages of society.

In the following pages you will find all the information needed to make you feel quite at your ease on every occasion - information which will solve for you all those little problems which are met with in the ordinary social round.

Study this little book, and when you have mastered its contents, put them into practice. You'll be rewarded by a feeling of poise and confidence, and the knowledge that you are popular with all with whom you come in contact - that you are what is known as "a social success."

WHEN YOU ENTERTAIN

WHEN YOU ENTERTAIN

Your first duty as a hostess is to see that your guests enjoy themselves. So that you may be able to give all your attention to them from the moment of their arrival, do see that your preparations are as complete as possible beforehand. This will avoid any fuss and confusion, too.

You will never make a good hostess unless you can forget yourself - your own likes and dislikes - for the time being and concentrate on putting your guests at their ease and seeing that they have a good time.

Introductions

In order to set the conversational ball rolling, all new-comers should be introduced to any of the company they may not know already. At a large dinner party, however, it is only necessary to introduce those who will sit next to each other.

When introducing a man and a woman, you should always "ask her permission" to make the introduction, thus: "Miss Blank, may I introduce Mr. Blink?"

If you were introducing two people of the same sex, you would introduce the less socially important to the more important; the younger to the elder, or the unmarried to the married "Mrs. Green, allow me to introduce Miss Brown." But remember that rank comes before age or the married state in social importance.

Preparing for a Little Dinner Party

There is a golden rule for giving a dinner party - never attempt anything more elaborate than you can comfortably manage. You will only be anxious lest any hitch should occur, and you'll be in no fit state to play the part of hostess as it should be played - with geniality and unruffled calm.

So, if you're expecting six guests to dinner, and you have only one little maid - possibly untrained - don't attempt a five or six course meal, expecting her to wash up, wait at table, and see to everything in kitchen and dining-room. Far better have a simple dinner which won't strain your resources.

A meal which goes off without a hitch is much more appreciated than an elaborate affair with awful pauses between the courses, or a crash of crockery outside the dining-room door when your flustered little maid lets drop the most important course on the floor!

Setting the Table

Don't overload your dinner table. If you do, you'll find that, when everyone is seated, things will constantly have to be moved about to make room for the various dishes to be set on the table. If your dinner table has been properly laid, nothing should have to be moved once people are seated.

> Small individual pepper pots and salt cellars at each corner of the table are handier than heavy cruet stands which have to be passed up and down the table.

When laying the covers, the first implements to be used should be placed at the outside, with the cutting edges of the knives turned inwards. So, if you are having soup, fish, meat and a sweet, place a soup spoon at the right side - at the outside - a fish knife next - with its fork on the left; inside these a steel knife, with its fork on the left. At the top of the cover, lay a dessert spoon for the sweet, with its handle towards the right, and beneath it, a dessert fork - handle towards the left.

Some people prefer, however, to have nothing at the top of the cover, and in this case, the dessert spoon and fork are placed inside the other implements, to the right and left respectively.

The glasses you will need, of course, depend upon what wines you are going to serve, but, as a general rule, put a tumbler, a wine, claret, or hock glass, and a port glass, in a little group, immediately to the right of each cover, and about nine inches in from the edge of the table.

Table napkins can be folded according to taste, but modern hostesses, who are more and more inclined towards simplicity, prefer to keep them folded flat, exactly as they come from the laundry, laying one for each cover, on which is placed a roll or piece of bread, cut fairly thick.

By the way, never refer to a table napkin as a "serviette." This term is now considered very old-fashioned.

A Splendid Idea for Serving

Up-to-date hostesses are more and more adopting the practice of having dishes carved at the sideboard or dumb waiter, or - whenever this is possible - having the dish handed round so that each guest can help himself.

This is a splendid idea, for it is often difficult for the host to give his mind to his guests while struggling with a refractory bird under the gaze of everybody at the table; or for a hostess to keep the conversation going while at the same time trying to serve two or more sweets.

Often, too, soup and sweets are served in little individual dishes - another good idea, as these can be prepared in the kitchen beforehand.

Preparations for Dessert

Now to the dessert, put all your fruit, nuts, etc., on to fruit dishes, and place on a side table in the dining-room.

Allow a dessert plate for each guest, on which is a dainty doily, a finger bowl half full of cold water, and a silver dessert knife and fork on either side of the bowl. You can, if you like, put a tiny piece of cut lemon floating in the water.

Bon-bon dishes containing salted almonds, olives, or sweets should be placed on the table beforehand.

Don't Make the Fatal Mistake

Wine should never by placed on the table; it should stand ready on the sideboard - decanted where necessary.

But don't make the mistake of opening up champagne or sparkling wines! If you do, they'll be flat by the time you are ready for them, of course.

As regards the wines to choose for your dinner party, this naturally depends upon the formality or informality of the occasion, your own and your guests' tastes, and last, but not least, upon how much you are prepared to spend.

The Correct Way
But for a modest little dinner party, just a choice of white or red wine (Burgundy or Claret, and Graves or Sauternes) is sufficient.

If you want to "go the whole hog,"
you can have:
cocktails or sherry in the drawing-room
before dinner;
sherry with the soup
(unless offered before dinner);
a white wine with the fish,
with a red wine, such as Burgundy, to follow
Port accompanies the dessert
Liqueurs accompany the coffee

You could offer whisky as an alternative and you should always have water, lemonade or mineral water handy for those who don't drink wines.

When Your Guests Arrive

At a formal dinner party, the host and hostess receive their guests in the drawing-room when they have shed their wraps. But in these days of domestic help shortage, very often the hostess escorts the lady guests to a bedroom which has been set apart as a cloak-room, while the host shows the men where to hang their hats and coats.

When all the guest are assembled, dinner should be announced; the parlourmaid comes to the door of the drawing-room and says: *"Dinner is served, Madam"*. The gong is only used for family meals nowadays.

Nowadays, except at very formal dinner parties, the host or hostess generally leads the way in to dinner, leaving the guests to follow as they please.

Seating Arrangements

Most hostesses, to ensure the party being well "mixed" at the dinner table, write out little "place-cards" beforehand. One is then placed on each cover, and the guests easily find their own places. Then the hostess should sit down, as the men will wait until she has done so before they seat themselves.

In placing guests, a hostess should arrange for the chief lady guest to sit at her husband's right, and the principal male guest at her right.
It looks so bad if there is a scramble to find chairs.

Serving the Wine
It is quite correct for the host to serve the wine, though if a butler or more than one maid is available to wait at table, one of them can do it.

Serving the Food
At a small dinner party - say six or eight people - the principal lady guest should be served first, then the lady on the host's left hand, and then all the other ladies in turn - including members of the household - next, the principal man guest, followed by the rest of the men, and the host last.
For a large party, serve the two principal ladies first. The maid should stand at the left of the host or hostess (whichever of them is serving) - ready to take each plate as it is filled.
She should place it in front of the guest, always standing at his or her left side to do so. At the same time, she should hand round one vegetable or gravy or sauce and the second vegetable, etc.,

when all the carving has been done.

You should tell your maid to be on the look out to see if any guest requires more vegetables, or bread or a second helping.

If you are giving an elaborate dinner, it is quite unnecessary to offer second helpings, though you could do so if your dinner only consisted of three or four courses. Never offer two helpings of soup.

Conversation at the Table

A hostess should divide her conversation more or less equally between her right and left-hand neighbours, although, at a small table, the talk is very often general. If she sees that any of her guests seem to be getting left out in the cold, she should try to draw them into the conversation, if she can do so without "shouting across" a number of other diners.

The Dessert Stage

When the dessert stage is reached, all remaining silver, cutlery, cruets and all glasses, except those for port, should be removed from the table.

All pieces of bread and crumbs should be taken up. The best way of doing this is for your maid to sweep them deftly on to a small tray, using a clean, crumpled-up napkin for the purpose.

She should then set the fruit on the table - one or two dishes opposite the host, and one or more opposite the hostess - and a dessert plate - ready set out with finger bowl, dessert knife and fork, as previously described, in front of each guest.

The fruit is then circulated round the table quite informally, and the port is taken round, either by the host or the waitress.

A hostess shouldn't finish eating any course before her guests, so she may have to spin out her portion a little!

Leaving the Men

When the hostess sees that all her guests have finished, she must "catch the eye" of her principal lady guest, who will be on the look out for this signal to rise. The hostess can, if she likes, murmur something such as, "Well, shall we go to the drawing-room?" but it isn't necessary to say anything at all.

As the hostess rises, all the other guests will follow suit, and the host or the man nearest to the door will open it for the ladies to pass out, leaving the men for a further talk, and possibly another round of port!

Coffee

Coffee is nearly always served in the drawing-room, after an interval of a few minutes.

Cups should be about three-quarters full, and should be handed on a fairly large tray, with milk and sugar, to which the guests help themselves. The men (if they are still in the dining-room) have theirs served there in the same way.

Some hostesses have coffee served at the dining-room table, at the end of dessert, and this is the best method if you wish liqueurs to accompany it.

In this case, the coffee can be handed round ready poured out, or it can be made in a percolator on the table and poured out by the hostess and carried round on a small tray to each guest in turn - offering milk and sugar at the same time.

Throughout the evening the hostess should try not to let any one person or group of people monopolise her. She should divide her favours equally among her guests as far as possible.

> Unless cards or some other form of entertainment is provided, the guests will probably leave about 10.30 or 11.00.

When You Have No Maid

Don't let it prevent you from giving a little dinner party should you have no maid to wait at table. There is no reason why it shouldn't go off without a hitch if you keep all the arrangements very simple. Don't attempt many courses. Have everything cold, or at most one hot course, such as a roast. You will find it much easier to have grapefruit as a first course, which can be placed ready on the table.

If you want a fish course, why not have a cold fish salad, or salmon mayonnaise?

When plates have to be changed, remove them yourself, or if you have a daughter, let her do it.

Do not let all the family jump up and rush about, it will only make the guests feel uncomfortable. Everything should be done as quietly, and with as little fuss, as possible.

When carving the joint or bird, it is better to do it at the table, so that the plates can be passed round from hand to hand. Set the vegetables opposite the hostess, who can either help the guests herself, or circulate the vegetable dishes.

The sweet should, if possible, be one which can be left ready to serve.

Dinner over, the hostess should conduct her guests to the drawing-room and leave the washing-up and clearing away until they have gone, unless she has a daughter who can unobtrusively slip out and put things away once the guests are settled in the drawing-room.

WHEN YOU GO TO A DANCE

WHEN YOU GO TO A DANCE

There are several different types of dances; there is the public subscription dance, to which anyone who cares to pay for a ticket can go; there is the private subscription dance, to which you must have an invitation, but for which you have to pay; then there is very often dancing at an hotel or restaurant for which you merely pay at the door and walk in.

There is also the formal private dance, and the little informal private dance to the gramophone or wireless.

If you go to a public or private subscription dance in a party, it is usual for everyone to pay for his or her own ticket, unless a man asks a particular girl to join the party as his partner, in which case he generally pays for her.

> If a girl asks a man to partner her for the evening, she should always pay for her own ticket.

Should you be asked as a guest by an older woman who is "taking a party" to a subscription dance, you must treat her as your hostess throughout the evening, and thank her before you leave for her hospitality. If she asks you to bring a partner with you, don't forget to let him know that you are both guests of your hostess, and he should have at least one duty dance with each of the ladies of the party.

Mix Well

You, on your part, should dance with the other men in the party, and not exclusively with your own partner, for the whole object in making up a party for a dance is that everyone should "mix well" and be jolly and sociable together.

The Official Hostess

When you go to a private subscription dance, you may quite likely find that there is an official "hostess." If so, you should go up and shake hands with her on arrival, introducing your partner to her, and at the end of the evening you should both go and take leave of her, congratulating her on the success of the evening, or some other suitable and appreciative remark.

The small private dance has no special rules of etiquette connected with it, beyond the ordinary good manners of civilised society - greeting your hostess on arrival, and thanking her afterwards and so on.

But suppose you have an invitation to a large private dance, and that, up to now, you have only been to subscription or club dances or little "hops"; perhaps you'll feel a little nervous and uncertain about the etiquette for this kind of occasion.

A Large Private Dance ~ a few helpful hints

When you arrive at the house, don't ask if your hostess is at home, but just walk in as soon as the door is opened.

After you have left your wrap in the cloak-room, make your way to where your hostess is receiving her guests.

At most private dances the guests' names are announced. When this is done, a servant will ask your name, which you should repeat quite clearly and audibly, saying whether "Mrs." or "Miss," so that she knows how to announce you.

As your name is called out, walk forward, fairly slowly and smiling pleasantly, and shake hands with your hostess.

After you have exchanged a few words, pass on into the ballroom - unless, of course, she keeps you back to introduce some partners, or hands you over to someone else.

If you have come with a "partner" of your own (which you should never do unless specifically asked to) don't let him monopolise you for the entire evening. It is expected of both of you to mix with the other guests to a certain extent.

Politeness Pays

Be pleasant and polite to all your partners - whether they are young and handsome, or elderly and boring! And, whatever you do, don't make the mistake of passing catty or critical remarks about the other dancers, the band, or any of the arrangements. Besides being very bad form, you never know whether remarks of that kind will be overheard or passed on to your hostess - or the person to whom you are talking may turn out to be relation or intimate friend of the son or daughter of the house!

Fall in with the arrangements made for the guests and enter into the spirit of the evening.

A Sit-down Supper

If there is a sit-down supper, there may be a plan of the tables, or place-cards showing you where you are to sit, so don't go off and sit somewhere else - even if the most attractive young man does try to lure you away to another table.

If you do, someone else will be left wandering about looking for a seat, and your hostess will have all the worry of re-arranging things.
If toasts are drunk - at a twenty-first birthday dance, for instance - rise when the toast is proposed.

When it is time to leave, seek out your hostess (and, if possible, any member of her family, such as a son or daughter for whom the dance is being given) and thank them prettily, saying how much you have enjoyed yourself.
As soon as you have said good-bye, fetch your cloak and take your departure.

After a dance of this kind, cards should be left with your hostess within a week or ten days.

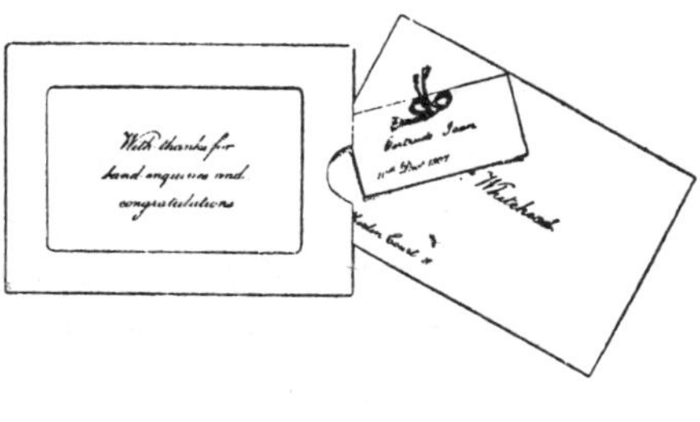

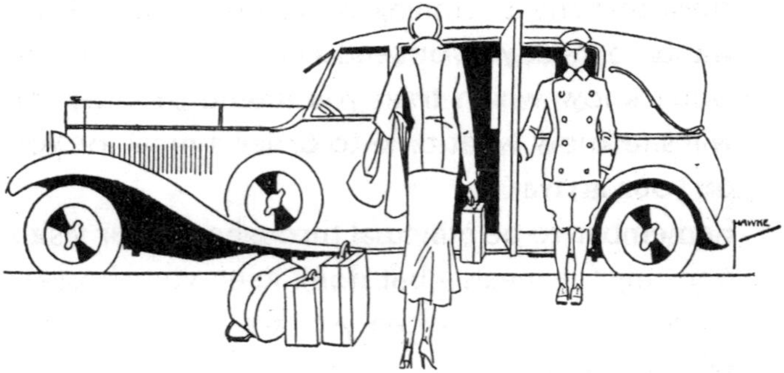

GOING AWAY TO STAY

GOING AWAY TO STAY

If you receive an invitation to stay with friends, do be very definite about the time of your arrival. It is most irritating for a hostess to be told by a guest that she is "coming in the afternoon." If she wants to meet you, or send a car to meet you, she won't know which train you intend to take; nor will she know what time to order a meal for you on your arrival.

Remember to be punctual throughout your visit - not only for meals - but don't keep your hostess waiting in the hall when you are going out anywhere together.

What clothes you will need to pack for your visit depends on the kind of place to which you are going - town, country or seaside.

For a visit to the country, you should equip yourself with sensible shoes, "tweedy" clothes, a mackintosh, and something to change into in the evenings.

You can leave behind your high-heeled street shoes, and smart town clothes, but pack an evening dress, because there is no place where they don't dance *sometimes* and country people "dress" quite as much as townsfolk for evening affairs.

If your visit is to the town, you can take with you anything smart and suitable to the type of visit.

But whether you are bound for town or country, don't take a greater quantity of luggage than the length of your stay demands.

It is both ridiculous and unnecessary to arrive with a large trunk for a week's visit, and it may make your hostess alarmed lest you intend to stay for a month!

Ask

If you are in doubt as to what kind of clothes to put on, ask your hostess. It will look more dignified than a hasty rush upstairs to change when you find that you've arrayed yourself in your glad rags and that the rest of the party is in tweeds!

Tidy

If you are staying in a house where there are plenty of servants, it doesn't mean that you can go out leaving your room like the bargain counter at the sales! Keep your room neat and tidy, and don't leave anything lying about for someone else to clear up after you.

Offer Help

Remember that a guest makes additional work for the maids in any case. Offer to help in the house if you think your hostess would be glad of it, and, even in a house where the mistress does not do any housework herself, remember that she has her hands full with ordering and superintending in the mornings, so amuse yourself until lunch time.

Very likely, though, you will be able to help your hostess by arranging flowers, posting letters, or small shopping commissions.

A Note of Thanks

As soon as possible after your return home, you should write and thank your hostess for your visit - it is not enough to thank her verbally when you leave, though you must do this as well, of course.

The Question of Tips ~ a few helpful hints

Treat servants with politeness and consideration, and before you leave, tip those who have served you personally in any way.
Girls are not expected to give large tips, so here are a few suggestions to guide you:

For a week-end
2s. to 2s. 6d. each to parlourmaid and housemaid.
For a week to a fortnight:
2s. 6d. to 3s. to each maid.
For longer than a fortnight: from 3s. to 5s. each.

The cook
The cook need not be tipped - unless she is a cook-general.

The chauffeur
If there is a chauffeur who has met you at the station, or driven you about during your stay, you can give him half-a-crown or more on leaving.

All tipping should be done personally if possible, as it is much more appreciated if a few words of thanks are added, such as: "Thank you very much for what you have done for me" ... etc. If you cannot find the maid who has done your room during your stay, you can leave the tip on the dressing-table.

Tipping sometimes puzzles an inexperienced traveller. The best way of reckoning how much you ought to distribute in tips is to take a tenth of the amount of your bill.

HOTEL ETIQUETTE

HOTEL ETIQUETTE

When you are going to stay at an hotel, it is as well to book your room beforehand, stating whether it is a double or single one you require and giving the exact dates of your stay if possible.

Before booking your rooms, it is wise to ask for the tariff if not already known, or you might find when too late that the prices charged were beyond your means!

On Arrival

When you arrive, the hotel porter will relieve you of your baggage and you should walk straight in and go to the reception office, where you will be told the number of your room and given your key. Sign your name in the visitors' book, either immediately or soon after arrival - putting the word "Mrs." or "Miss" before your name. If a husband and wife are travelling together, the husband signs for himself and his wife, thus: "Mr. and Mrs. Charles

Smith." When leaving your room, it is better to lock it - certainly if you are going out - and to deposit the key with the reception clerk.

Meals

Inquire the times at which meals are served if you do not see a notice displayed which gives these. Don't make the mistake of rushing down the minute the gong sounds - or on the tick of the dinner-hour; always wait two or three minutes first. You can wear a hat, or not, just as you like, for breakfast, lunch and tea. At dinner, a simple dinner frock, or a pretty afternoon frock is correct for any but very smart hotels.

If you want calling earlier than usual, ask the chambermaid, or the reception clerk will arrange this for you should you arrive after the chambermaid has gone off duty.

When you enter the dining-room for your first meal, the head waiter will come forward and show you which table to sit at and this table will be reserved for you for the remainder of your stay.

Leaving

When you are leaving, give notice at the reception office the night before, or before midday if you are leaving late in the day. At the same time, ask for your bill to be in readiness, so that you aren't kept waiting for it.

Tipping sometimes puzzles an inexperienced traveller. The best way of reckoning how much you ought to distribute in tips is to take a tenth of the amount of your bill, and divide this sum among the hotel staff who have given you any service.

The head waiter should receive a slightly larger tip than the others. Your own waiter and the chambermaid should receive about equal tips, and smaller amounts could be given to the luggage porter or others who have served you.

Hand your tips to the waiters at the end of your last meal, and ring for the chambermaid and give her hers just before you leave your room.

The other hotel servants can be tipped as you are about to leave - you need not worry that you will not see them, they are sure to be on the look out for you!

Pay your bill at the office just before you go, but it is not the thing to tip the reception clerk.

WHEN YOU GO ABROAD

WHEN YOU GO ABROAD

When you are in a foreign country, do remember that you are, in a small way, an ambassador for your own country. By your courteous (or otherwise) behaviour will your poor countrymen be judged. English people abroad are, unfortunately, so very apt to adopt a haughty, truculent air; to walk about the capitals of Europe in clothes which they would only consider fit for the beach or country lanes at home, and, generally to behave themselves as though all the foreigners with whom they come in contact were either deaf of mentally deficient. Small wonder that in many places abroad we are known as "those mad English," or by other names even more unkind.

Reputation

Next time you go abroad, then, make up your mind that you will do something to gain a reputation for yourself and for your fellow Britishers for courtesy and good manners, and you will find that, incidentally, you will enjoy your holiday far more, and will find that things go much more smoothly.

Passport

Before you start, be sure that your passport is in order. If you have not already a passport, you must set about getting one in good time. Call or write to the Passport Office for the form to fill in.
When you have filled in the particulars you must take the form to a Justice of the Peace, a doctor, solicitor or clergyman for his signature. He will vouch that the form is correctly filled in, take it to someone whom you know, if possible.

> Have your photograph taken according to the passport requirements.

When filling in your passport form, it is as well to ask for a visa for as many countries as possible, since when travelling, one frequently crosses the frontier of several countries, and your passport must include any country over who frontier you step or you may find yourself in difficulties!
If you prefer it, it is possible to secure a passport through your bank, and this is often simpler for people who do not live in London.

Money

See that you have a sufficient supply of money, and a certain sum in the currency of the country to which you are going. You can get money changed at any bank, or travel agency, or at any of the bureaux de change at the London main line stations. Should you overlook this, though, the purser on the boat on which you cross can generally change money for you.

It is just as well not to travel with a very large sum of money on you, so get your bank or travel agency to give you a "traveller's cheque" or "letter of credit," so that you can draw the money as required from an agency or bank on your arrival at your destination.

Luggage Matters

See that your luggage is in good condition and adequately labelled. It will have to undergo fairly rough handling on boat and train, remember. It is best to insure your luggage before starting; this can be done either through a travel agency, an insurance company or the railway company.

The kind of clothes you will require to take will depend entirely upon the type of holiday you are planning. In general, on the Continent dress is not quite so formal as in England, and, at any quiet hotel, full evening dress will not be found necessary. But at many of the casinos it is compulsory, and it is always as well to take one evening dress if possible, unless you are going quite "into the wilds."

Knowing the Language

As a general rule, it is not necessary to know the language of the country to which you are going, if you are keeping more or less to the beaten tracks, though it is an undoubted advantage to be able to speak and understand at least a smattering. Also, you will enjoy and appreciate everything very much more, get on better with the people, and find travelling and getting about so much easier if you have taken the trouble to learn a certain amount of the language before you start.

There are many handy little phrase-books which give phrases together with the pronunciation, and armed with one of these and a dictionary, it is wonderful how much one can pick up, even in a short time.

Tipping When Travelling

Tipping, generally speaking, is very much more general on the Continent than it is in this country. Theatre attendants, guides, purveyors of bathing tents - nearly everyone who renders you any kind of service expects a tip in addition to the normal amount charged.

Service Charge

The recognised tip is ten per cent of the charge made, this is quite adequate, and it is unnecessary to pay more. On your hotel bill you will most probably find ten per cent for "Service" as one of the items, and when this is so, no additional tipping of the staff need be done.

Foreigners are more ceremonious in their manners than are English people. So, when you go into the dining-room of your hotel for meals, you will probably find that your fellow guests bow to you, and those nearest may even wish you good morning, even though they have not spoken to you before. Don't be stiff and awkward, but reply in the same courteous spirit.

"When in Rome ..."
When abroad, it is always best to follow, as far as reasonable, the customs of the country in which you find yourself.

> Don't, for instance, be one of those tiresome people who loudly demand eggs and bacon for breakfast when rolls and coffee are provided. It is this kind of person who gets us the reputation for being insular and eccentric!

When your stay is over, and you pack up for the homeward journey, do remember that any treasures you may have collected will have to pass through the Customs. If you have anything to declare, don't hesitate to do so - the duty is quite small, as a rule, and the penalties for disobeying the regulations are very heavy. If you are not sure what articles are dutiable, ask the Customs official for a list.

TIPS ON TABLE MANNERS

TIPS ON TABLE MANNERS

There must have been a moment in all our lives when we were suddenly confronted with a new and strange dish, and we realised with panic that we didn't know how to tackle it!
Little surprises are bound to occur from time to time, and it is as well to know how various luxury dishes are served and eaten.

General Rules

As a general rule, you will find that the "tool" you are expected to use first is placed at the outside of the cover, and the others are arranged inwards, in the order in which the dishes come. But a few additional tips will be necessary if you want to be quite certain of the correct procedure.

Hors d'oeuvres

Generally, a special silver knife and fork are placed on your plate - if not, they will be found at the outside of your cover. Help yourself, with the implements provided, to a little of any of the dishes you fancy. In a restaurant the waiters often serve you, asking you which you will like.

Olives

These are eaten with the fingers. They are sometimes included with the hors d'oeuvres.

Caviare

This is served with toast. Spread a little on the toast with the small knife provided and eat with the fingers. Sometimes the caviare is already spread on small rounds of toast; in this case, eat it with the small knife and fork provided.

Grapefruit

This is served in glass holders, and is ready cut round the edges. It is eaten with a small spoon.

Melon

This is served in slices, and sugar is sprinkled over. Sometimes ground ginger is offered, but do not take this if you do not care for ginger. Melon is eaten with a dessert spoon, the fruit being held steady on the plate with the left hand.

Oysters

These are served with brown bread and butter, slices of lemon and several sorts of pepper. Squeeze a little lemon juice over, and take a little pepper - if you decide on the "red pepper," remember it is very hot! Steady the shell with your left hand and lift the oyster out with the small fork provided, and put it whole into your mouth.

Soup

This is eaten with the spoon you will find placed at your right hand, at the outside of the cover. Always drink soup from the side of the spoon, never from the tip. If there are pieces of meat or vegetables which you cannot manage in this way, leave them. They are only intended for flavouring anyway. If croutons (little cubes of fried bread) are served with soup, take a few and put them in your soup, but never break up your own bread and put it in your soup plate. You can tip your plate, provided you tilt it away from you, but do not drain it to the very dregs.

Fish

A silver fish knife and fork will be found to right and left, outside the other implements. It is correct to use these for any fish dish. When eating whitebait, remember that the whole of the fish is eaten, you are not expected to trim off the heads and tails!

Entrees

These are generally eaten with a fork if they are the soft variety. If they seem to need a knife - as with cutlets, sweetbreads, etc., you will be quite correct in using a knife as well.

Curry

Eat this with a spoon and fork, or with a fork alone if it is dry.

Joints, Game and Poultry

Don't start eating these until you are served with vegetables, appropriate sauces, gravy, or salad. Don't try to scrape every morsel of meat from the bones of poultry or game.

Salad

This is very often served with poultry or game instead of a second vegetable. If it is served on a small plate, it will be placed at your side, and you eat it direct from this: do not empty it on to your dinner plate.

Peas

These are eaten with a knife and fork, the peas being pressed on to the fork with the aid of the knife.

> Avoid spiking the peas with the fork, or using the latter as a shovel to scoop up the peas, which looks ugly and clumsy.

Asparagus

This is most often served as a separate course, with melted butter or sauce. Lift up each spike in your right hand, dip the head in the sauce and bite off the soft part. Do not attempt to eat the hard butts. Where asparagus holders are provided, pick up each spike with these, and proceed as already described. Sometimes finger bowls are placed on the table with the asparagus. When this is done dip the tips of your right-hand fingers in the water and wipe them on your table napkin.

Artichokes

Generally served as a separate course. When handed round, take one from the dish with the spoon provided. Then, with the fingers, break off each leaf, dip the soft, fleshy end into the sauce served with them and bite off this soft part leaving the rough part on the side of your plate.

Sweets, Ices

Sweets are eaten with a fork if at all possible. If too liquid, with a spoon and fork. Never eat a sweet with the spoon only, except in the case of ices, which are eaten with a small spoon provided. Petits fours, which often accompany the sweet course at restaurants, are eaten with the fingers.

The Dessert ~ a few helpful hints

When the dessert course arrives, a plate will be placed in front of you on which you will find a finger bowl resting on a small doily, with a silver knife and fork on each side of it.

First quietly transfer the knife and fork to the table on either side of your dessert plate, and then lift the finger bowl and put it on the table, with its doily under it, on your left side and about the same distance from the edge of the table as your wine-glass occupies on your right hand.
Do this quite quietly and unobtrusively.

Most dessert fruits should be peeled: apples and oranges, and other fairly hard fruits are held in the left hand and peeled with the dessert knife.

Soft, juicy fruits, such as peaches or plums, should be held with the fork while peeled with the knife.

Cherries, grapes and other small fruits are eaten with the fingers, and the skin, pips or stones daintily removed with the fingers.

Don't be surprised if your dinner partner offers to peel your fruit or crack some nuts for you. This is a little courtesy, which is often offered by a well-mannered man to the lady he has 'taken in' to dinner.
Accept the little compliment graciously unless, of course, you wish to refuse the dessert course altogether.

Cheese

When eating cheese, cut off small portions with your knife and place one at a time on a biscuit or piece of bread and bite off a mouthful. Old-fashioned people still occasionally eating cheese with a knife, this is quite wrong nowadays. It is a fashion which went out with the last century.

Finger Bowls

When you have finished, dip the tips of your fingers only in your finger bowl and wipe them daintily on your dinner napkin. The whole proceeding should be done very unobtrusively: the girl who makes the mistake of thinking that the finger bowl is to be used to "wash her hands in" and her table napkin as a towel, is apt to be looked at askance by the other diners!

As soon as you sit down to table, you should have unfolded your table napkin and put it across your knee.

When dessert is over, crumple it up loosely and place it on the table beside you. Never fold up your table napkin, unless you are actually staying in the house where the meal is taken, and even then, not at a formal dinner party, unless your hostess does so.

Wines

Cocktails or sherry are generally served in the drawing-room (in a private house) or in the lounge (at a restaurant) before going in to dinner. You need not take either unless you like.

Cocktails are generally served with an olive or cherry on a little stick. These are eaten from the stick, but you can leave them if you like.

Other wines are served with the different courses - sherry with the soup, and so on.

Or there may simply be one or two different wines to choose from.

It is perfectly correct to refuse any you do not care for and it is much safer not to 'mix your drinks' unless you are very certain how much you can take!

When the glass is half empty, the waiter, or your host, will probably automatically replenish it, but you can stop him if you do not wish for any more. Liqueurs are sometimes served with the coffee, but, here again, it is quite optional for you to refuse.

Cigarettes are occasionally handed round between the courses nowadays - not, however, until after the meat courses are finished. You can take one if you wish, but even smokers often do not care to smoke during a meal, so there is no need at all to do so, if you do not wish. Guests should never produce their own cigarettes during dinner.

Those Who Serve

Nothing should be said to the servants waiting at the table, except in response to a definite question - "Will you take a little more wine, madam?"

obviously requires "Yes, please", or "No, thank you" in reply, but it isn't necessary to say "thank you" to the servant when she hands you dishes in the ordinary course of her waiting duties, nor does any trained servant expect this.

Needless to say, all servants, whether in your own, or in someone else's house should be treated with quiet courtesy, and they will of course, appreciate a few kindly words now and then, but the dining-room is not the place for this. Tips should not be given to any of the servants at a private dinner party.

RESTAURANT MEALS

RESTAURANT MEALS

Perhaps you have a "date" with your boy-friend to lunch or dine at a smart restaurant, and you are not very well up in restaurant etiquette? Well, here are one or two hints which will help you to acquit yourself like a woman of the world!

First of All - What to Wear
For lunch at smart restaurants, wear your nicest town outdoor clothes. You should be slick and well-groomed, but not flashy.
Leave your trailing chiffons in the wardrobe, and don't adorn yourself with a lot of jewellery. Dress rings (unless it is your engagement ring) aren't worn in the day-time nowadays, anyhow, and bracelets and other jewellery are out of place except in the evening. A necklace of beads or pearls and possibly ear-rings is all you should allow yourself. A small, smart hat is ideal for restaurant wear, and your gloves, shoes, stockings and handbag should be above reproach. If you use scent, it should be the merest suspicion.

Punctuality

Be reasonably punctual in meeting your escort. You needn't be before time, of course, but don't keep him waiting more than five minutes; so many girls think nothing of keeping a man waiting twenty minutes or half an hour, and then they are surprised when the poor fellow is rather chilly, and his cordiality is somewhat damped. Besides, he may very likely have booked a table for a certain time, and you will very likely find this has been given up to someone else, the head waiter having concluded that you weren't coming after all.

Entering the Dining-Room

When you go into the dining or grill room, the man should precede you, as he will arrange with the head waiter where you are to sit. When you arrive at your table, choose your seat and sit down - your escort, or the waiter will most likely pull out your chair for you. Now slip off your gloves, but don't remove your hat. Unfold your table napkin and place it on your knees.

Ordering the Meal

The waiter may hand you each a menu card, or he may hand one to your host only. Before you start suggesting a choice of food, find out whether your boy-friend intends to order the table d'hôte meal, or whether he prefers to order à la carte.

The table d'hôte is generally cheaper, and, of course, you don't want to run him into a big bill unless you are sure that he intends to entertain you regardless of expense!

If you only want a very light lunch, say so, and then you can pick out something à la carte, which will be more satisfactory to your host than allowing him to pay for an elaborate meal, of which you have only eaten, say, two courses. As you make your choice, tell your friend what you would like, and he will then order for both of you; don't give your order direct to the waiter.

As regards drinks, it is always as well to let the man choose - he can then suggest something according to the depth of his purse!

When the meal is over, it is your place to make a move to go. Whilst your host is settling the bill, gather up your wrap and gloves, so that you are ready by the time he is.

Offering to Pay

It is quite unnecessary for a girl to offer to pay her share when she has been asked out by a man - unless under some very special circumstances - for instance, a very wealthy or elderly woman who is dining with a young man, or an engaged couple who have come to this arrangement because the young man is not at all well off.

But it is better to let the man pay the bill and tactfully suggest afterwards that it should be a "fifty-fifty" arrangement. A man always feels it wounding to his dignity to have a woman guest wrangling in public over the the bill. In most cases, he asked you out because he wanted the pleasure of your company, and he expects to pay for it!

It is Only Good Manners

Do remember to thank him prettily. That is only good manners, and far too many girls, in their anxiety to seem sophisticated, think it is quite unnecessary to thank a man for his entertainment.

When You Dine Out

The same rules apply to dining as to lunching at a restaurant. If you are in any doubt as to whether your host will wear evening dress, do ask beforehand. It is much better to be sure than sorry, and you will both feel uncomfortable if you turn up in evening dress and he has not changed, or vice versa.

Don't bother to change ...

If he says *"don't bother to change,"* you can wear slightly more frivolous clothes than you would for a lunch - either a pretty semi-evening frock, or a coat and skirt with a fluffy blouse, and a small, smart hat; gloves, of course, and neat street shoes.

If it is an evening dress occasion, do not wear a hat, but slip on a cloak or coat over your frock, and wear evening shoes. Gloves are quite optional, except when you are going on to a very smart function afterwards, such as the opera, or an important dance.

When you arrive at the restaurant or hotel where you are dining, you can leave your wrap in the cloak-room, or you can go into the dining-room and put it over the back of your chair.

The Theatre

If you should be going on to a theatre after dinner, you can reserve your thanks till the end of the evening. Allow your host to precede you into the theatre, as he will have the tickets. Having found your seats, he will then stand aside for you to pass along to yours.

You should try to be punctual at a theatre for the sake of the rest of the audience, but if you do unfortunately arrive after the play has started, try to make your way to your seats as quietly as possible, with a whispered apology to those whom you have to push past.

When you arrive late at a concert, you should wait until the movement is finished before making your way to your seats. Always try to be very punctual when you go to the opera - late comers are frowned upon very heavily by opera "fans."

Public Dinners

When you go to a public dinner, the etiquette is much the same as for an ordinary dinner. Make certain first whether it is evening or morning dress. If the latter, you are expected to wear a hat - your coat can be left in the cloak-room.

There is sure to be a plan of the tables, and you should consult this to see where you are expected to sit. Be sure to bring with you your ticket or invitation card, whichever admits you to the dinner.

At a public dinner, the King's health is always drunk, and it is a very strict rule that there shall be no smoking until this has been done. When toasts are proposed, rise to your feet, and lift your glass as you will see others doing.

When the diners rise at the end of the dinner, you leave at once, unless there is dancing or a concert to follow. It is not necessary to take your leave of anyone, unless you are the personal guest of one of the company, when, of course, you will tender your thanks to him or her before leaving.

THE CUSTOM OF CALLING

THE CUSTOM OF CALLING

Calling is a custom which has died out to a great extent in the last few years, but everyone should know the laws which govern it, in case they find themselves in circles where it is still practised. In fact, there are occasions when everyone should do a little "pasteboard slinging," as it is irreverently called by some young moderns.

Cards

First of all, see that your visiting cards are just right.

There is a very definite standard for these, which must be conformed to if you wish to be correct. Cards should be plain white pasteboard with square corners. The proper size for a lady's card is 3¼ inches long and 2¼ inches deep.

The wording should be "engraved" in black. Don't, for the sake of economy, be tempted to have them "printed" - because it will give them a "commercial" look, and you will never be satisfied with them.

As to the wording, here again it is very important not to go wrong. Be sure you have the word Mrs. or Miss before your surname. If you're married, your husband's Christian name should come before your surname - Mrs. John Smith, or Mrs. John V. Smith.

If you are unmarried, have your cards engraved Miss Smith if you are the eldest or an only daughter; or Miss Mary Smith, if you have any older sisters. Girls living at home sometimes have their name printed on their mother's cards, just underneath her name.

The name is always on the centre of the card and the address in the lower left-hand corner. For some reason, it is not considered good form to have one's telephone number printed on visiting cards.

The Use of Visiting Cards

Having got your cards engraved, you must master the rules of their use. The married woman's problem is the only one which presents any difficulty, for she has to cope with her husband's cards as well as her own. But this isn't really at all complicated once she has mastered the rules which govern card etiquette.

WHY BE THIN?
Try my marvellous
Discovery FREE
I will fill out your Figure and give you rounded limbs and a perfectly shaped Bust. Send 3d. in stamps for postage, and I will send a package ENTIRELY FREE of charge or obligation.
My preparation is absolutely harmless, but marvellously effective. Send for Free Package Now to
NURSE ANDERSON
(Dept. S.S.2), 25 Hoghton St., Southport, Lancs.

Leaving your card ~ a few helpful hints

A couple not at home
When a married woman leaves cards on a married couple who are not at home, she leaves one of her own and two of her husband's. One of her husband's cards is for the lady of the house and one for her husband. Why doesn't the wife also leave two cards? "A woman never pays a call on a man" unless it is purely a business call.

A hostess at home
Supposing the hostess were at home, you would leave your husband's cards, but not your own. Cards represent the person whose name they bear, in this case your absent husband, but as you have paid your call in person, there is no need to leave your card as well.

Call on an unmarried woman or widow
When your call is on an unmarried woman or a widow, exactly the same rules apply, except that one of your husband's cards would be left instead of two.

Call on a bachelor
If you are calling on a bachelor who has his mother or sister living with him, you leave your cards according to the rules for calling on a married couple. The mother or sister keeping house for a bachelor "leaves cards" for him when she goes calling, as if they were a married couple.

Card Leaving for the Bachelor Girl

The unmarried girl's or widow's card-leaving is a simple business. She leaves one of her cards whenever she calls upon someone who is not at home. The only occasion upon which you leave cards - according to the rules already given - when the folk called upon are actually at home, is when you make or return a "first call" upon new-comers in your neighbourhood, or when you are the new-comer yourself.

This is for convenience's sake, so that the person called upon shall have your name and address for future reference.

> If you are a new-comer to a neighbourhood, you must wait until called upon by the people of the district: it is their privilege to make the first move.

Rules for Returning Calls

Calls should be returned within ten days or at the most a fortnight. The correct time for calling is in the afternoon, and never before three o'clock. When leaving cards upon someone who is not at home, just hand them to the maid, who will place them on a small tray kept in the hall.

If leaving your husband's cards at the end of a visit, don't hand them to your hostess, but place them on the hall table.

Never send in your cards by a maid to announce your arrival, except when making a business call.

If you are calling to inquire after an invalid, it is quite permissible to call at other than the formal hours for calling, and you should then write at the top of your cards the words:

"To inquire."

It is correct (though many people neglect this courtesy these days) to leave your cards on your hostess after a dinner party, or an At Home. In this case, it isn't necessary to ask if your hostess is at home - just hand in your cards at the door.

Such calls should be paid within a few days of the function, and should be made whether the invitation was accepted or refused.

LETTER-WRITING

LETTER-WRITING

It is very important to be able to write a good letter, for slovenly, untidy and careless letter-writing is discourteous to the recipient, and will probably put its writer at a disadvantage socially, while a badly expressed business letter can sometimes let one in for all sorts of trouble and misunderstanding.

Note-paper and Envelopes

First of all, see that your note-paper is all that it should be. It is considered very bad taste to indulge in flamboyant stationery, so beware of hectic coloured note-paper, embossed initials or scented paper!

Choose note-paper and envelopes of a quiet hue - either white, ivory, grey or dull blue, and have your address and telephone number stamped on it in plain lettering.

Good Form

Always date your letters, writing this either at the top left-hand corner, or immediately beneath the address.

Be sure to leave a good margins and write clearly and legibly. The form of your letters varies, according to whether they are written to business or tradespeople, or to intimate friends.

To shops or hotels

When writing to shops, or to hotels it is quite usual - though not necessary - to write in the third person. Write the date at the top of your note-paper and then plunge without any preliminary *Dear* ... into what you have to say, thus:

Mrs. Brown would be glad if the Manager would reserve her two single rooms for Friday and Saturday nights, October 10th and 11th.

For a Reference

To write about a servant's character:

Mrs. Brown would be very much obliged if Mrs. Robinson could tell her anything about the character and capabilities of Annie Smith, who has applied to her for the position of housemaid. Is she a good worker, neat and honest? Any other remarks Mrs. Robinson would care to make would be much appreciated.

Never sign your name to a letter in the third person, and beware of lapsing into

"I should very much appreciate anything further you may care to say, etc."

When giving dates, whether you are writing formal business letters, or letters to personal friends, always give both the day and the date:

I should be so pleased if you would come to a little party on Friday of next week, May 10th.

This often avoids embarrassment and confusion, if you forget to post your letter till the week-end and then your friend would wonder whether it was really that week you meant, or the one after; while if you simply wrote May 10th, and your figures were not absolutely clear, she might turn up on the wrong day, to your mutual inconvenience!

Formal or Informal

Always keep business letters strictly concise and formal. If not written in the third person, they should start *"Dear Sir"* or *"Dear Madam,"* and finish with *"Yours faithfully"*.

When writing to acquaintances - people whom you have met socially, but whom you do not know intimately - start *"Dear Mrs. Price,"* and end up *"Yours sincerely," "Sincerely yours,"* or - if you want to be a little more cordial: *"Yours very sincerely."*

Sign your Christian name or initials and then your surname - never sign yourself *"Mrs. Florence Martin,"* though, when writing a business letter to a person or firm, it is quite usual to put (Mrs.) or (Miss) in brackets just before your signature - simply for their convenience in replying to your letter. But never leave out the brackets, whatever you do.

When writing any social letter - except a formal invitation - do beware of using stilted, high-sounding phrases. Write quite naturally, just as you would talk. Don't write *"commence"* when you mean *"begin"* or *"residence"* when you mean *"house."*

Between Friends

After all, correspondence between friends is used only when conversation with them is impossible, and bright, chatty letters which speak of your personality are always much more welcome than a species of essay which might have been written by a complete stranger.

The Right Way with Envelopes

As regards the addressing of envelopes: begin about a third down from the top and, say, an inch from the left-hand edge.

If you are addressing a married woman, use her husband's Christian name or initials as well as her married surname: Mrs. John Ford, or Mrs. C.H. Ford. When writing to an unmarried girl, address her as Miss Wright, unless she is a younger daughter, or unless, for any reason, there is likely to be confusion - as, for instance, if she were staying at an hotel, where there might be more than one person with the same surname - you should then add her Christian name or initials.

Men should be addressed with their surname, preceded by their Christian name or initials, with the words Esq. added after the surname - except in the case of doctors, clergymen, or those of military or naval rank.

When you have addressed your envelope, seal the letter neatly and securely and please be sure to stick the stamp on the right way up and straight.

Post cards

Post cards should be written with discretion, nothing should be said that you or the recipient would mind being read by a third person. It is not necessary (or correct) to begin *"Dear So-and So"* on a post card; write the address and the date and then begin straight away with what you have to say. Omit the *"Yours sincerely,"* etc., at the end and simply sign your name or initials.

Telegrams

When sending telegrams, it is sufficient to use the shortest form of address which will be quite certain to reach the person to whom it is sent: omit the Mrs, Miss, or Esq., simply use Brown - or John Brown if there are two Mr. Browns in the same house - and sign your surname only - or your Christian name only if your telegram is to an intimate friend or relation.

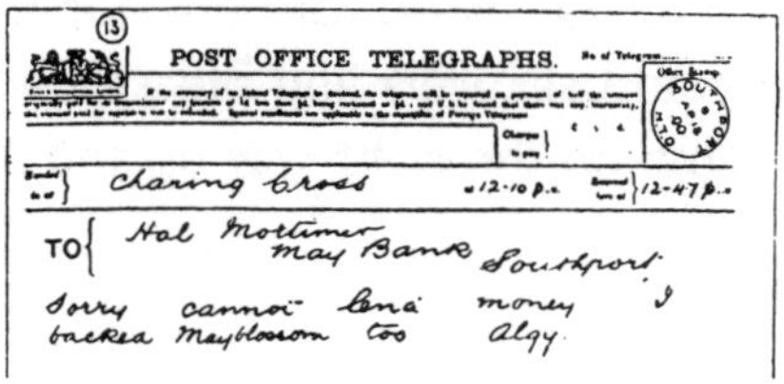
(13)
POST OFFICE TELEGRAPHS.
Charing Cross 12-10 p.m. 12-47 p.m.
TO { Hal Mortimer May Bank Southport.
Sorry cannot lend money I backed Mayblossom too Algy.

INVITATIONS

Invitations form rather a special branch of letter-writing, because, as general rule, they are both written and replied to in the "third person."

When issuing invitations to a wedding, a large dance, a reception or an At Home, a hostess generally has cards printed, merely writing in the name of each guest across the top in ink. Thus you might get an invitation to a private dance something like this:

Miss Mary Smith
Mrs. Wilfred Brown
AT HOME
Thursday, November 9th
R.S.V.P.
The Laurels
Grove Road
S.W.1.
Dancing 9-2

To this you would reply:

Miss Mary Smith has much pleasure in accepting Mrs. Wilfred Brown's kind invitation to a dance on Thursday, November 8th.

Nothing more, except your address at the top of the paper, and the date. Beware of making the common mistake of writing "... will have much pleasure in accepting" - this is incorrect. Never sign your name to any kind of letter written, like this, in the third person. The letters "R.S.V.P." indicate that a reply is expected, which should be sent to the address immediately below.

Refusing!

If you wish to refuse an invitation, you should write something on these lines:

Miss Mary Smith thanks Mrs. Brown for her kind invitation to her dance on Thursday, November 8th, but regrets that, owing to a previous engagement (or owing to illness, etc.), she is unable to accept.

Always give a reason if you have to refuse an invitation - it is very ill-bred indeed to refuse without giving any explanation.

Should you receive an invitation and at the foot of the card is printed these words:

"Orders and Decorations will be worn," do remember that this only refers to decorations actually conferred by the King.

It is a breach of etiquette not to wear any such decorations to which one is entitled, so see that your menfolk wear their war medals Do not fall into the error of decking yourself out with the Chairman's badge of any charitable association or club to which you may belong!

Always reply to invitations by return of post, or if this is impossible, as soon as you reasonably can. This is a common courtesy due to your hostess, who naturally wants to know how many guests to expect. Far too many people nowadays put off answering invitations for days, or even weeks - either from sheer laziness, or merely to see if some more attractive engagement turns up!

There's absolutely no excuse for this, and a girl who does so will soon find herself left out of things when gaieties are afoot.

Informal Invitations

Of course, invitations may take all kinds of different forms, but it is a perfectly safe rule to frame your reply in the same strain in which the invitation is received.

Supposing you get a friendly note asking you to tea, lunch or to play cards - you should reply by a note worded in the same style - and as soon as possible, please!

If you receive an invitation by word of mouth or by a telephone message while you are out, you can either reply by telephone or by an informal note - whichever is most convenient.

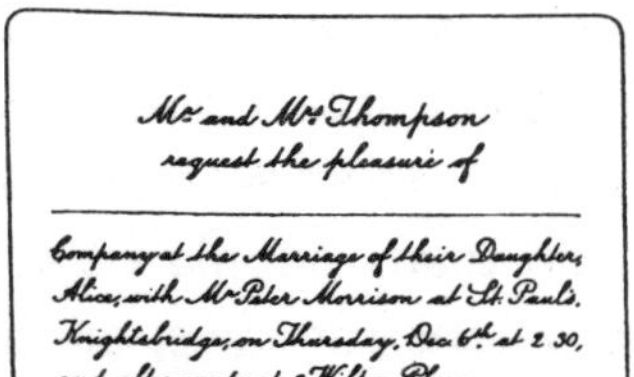

Mr. and Mrs. Thompson
request the pleasure of

Company at the Marriage of their Daughter, Alice, with Mr. Peter Morrison at St. Paul's, Knightsbridge, on Thursday, Dec. 6th at 2.30, and afterwards at 3 Wilton Place.

R.S.V.P.

The most usual thing is for the couple to go together to choose the ring, but it saves embarrassment if the man goes to the jeweller's first and explains what kind of ring is required, and the price he is prepared to pay. This will prevent the girl being shown rings and perhaps choosing one which may be quite beyond her fiancé's means.

ENGAGEMENTS AND WEDDINGS

ENGAGEMENTS AND WEDDINGS

When a couple become engaged, the man should at once call upon his fiancé's father - or nearest relative if he is not living - and ask for his sanction to the engagement.
It is absolutely necessary to obtain the parents' consent where the bride is under twenty-one, and in any case it is only common politeness to ensure that the girl's father and mother are the first to hear of such an important event.

The Interview

When the young man has an interview with his prospective father-in-law, it is expected of him to explain his financial circumstances and business prospects, so as to reassure the girl's father that he is in a position to keep his daughter. The man is expected to give his fiancé an engagement ring, and before doing this, he should ask her what type of stone and setting she prefers.

The Jeweller

The most usual thing is for the couple to go together to choose it, but it saves embarrassment if the man goes to the jeweller's first and explains what kind of ring is required, and the price he is prepared to pay. This will prevent the girl being shown rings and perhaps choosing one which may be quite beyond her fiancé's means, when he might feel awkward if he had to tell her so, or "haggle" about the price in front of her!

The Announcement

If it is desired to announce the engagement in the papers, a notice something in this style should be inserted:

"An engagement has been arranged between Mr. Alfred Henry Brown, son of Mr. and Mrs. Francis Brown, of The Gables, Windy Road, Blackpool, and Mary Eleanor, elder daughter of Captain and Mrs. Harold Stokes, of 63, Dashwood Place, London, S.W.1."

If the date of the wedding has already been arranged, it can, if desired, be included in the engagement announcement.

Whether the engagement is announced in the Press or not, the girl and her mother should write short notes to their relations and near friends informing them of it, while the man on his side should do the same with his relations and friends.

As soon as the engagement has been recognised by the girl's parents, the prospective "in-laws" will, of course, wish to meet each other, if they have not already done so.

There is no special rule of etiquette for this, but it is more usual for the young man's people to make the first move. They would write a friendly letter to the girl or her mother, asking them to come and see them, or stay with them if they lived at a distance.

The girl should never accept an invitation to his home from the young man unless it is backed up by an invitation from his mother as well.

When the engagement becomes known, friends and relations will write and congratulate the young couple. Strictly speaking, they should only "congratulate" the man - their letters to the girl should simply be to "wish her happiness."

Letters of congratulations should be replied to as they are received. Quite a short note of thanks is sufficient.

Happy Engagements

A girl's engagement days should be the happiest in her life, so it is important that she should avoid disagreements between herself and her fiancé, or her own and his people.

> Many engagements come to grief because the young couple expect each other to abandon all their former interests once they become engaged. It is a mistake to drop all your friends.

A girl should try not to let her happiness make her selfish, with her own people, or in the claims she makes on the time of her fiancé.

Her mother and father will not expect her to devote as much of her time to them now that she is engaged, but she should try to make up to them for this by being extra thoughtful when she is with them. Also, the young man's people will want to see something of their son before he leaves them for a home of his own.

A Wholesome Change of Company

If you spend your entire time in each other's company, you will get "stale," and the first bliss of engagement will wear off more quickly than if you indulged in a little wholesome change of company now and again. Your friends are apt to be hurt if you drop them like hot coals the minute "Mr. Right" comes along! They may not be ready to be "picked up" again, when you discover that you can't do without friends even if you have a husband!

Another Mistake

A mistake so many girls make is to demand that their fiancé shall give up his sports and masculine pursuits as soon as the engagement ring is in place.

Share

The ideal state of affairs is, of course, where both are keen on some sport which they can share, but where the man is a rugger or cricket fan, for instance, it is a great pity to deprive him of the benefit which he will get from the exercise, and he will appreciate your company all the more if you agree to devote perhaps one afternoon a week to your respective sports or hobbies.

"A Wedding has been Arranged"

When the date of the wedding has been fixed, it is time to think about sending out the invitations. These are always printed on a double sheet of note-paper. Any good stationer will advise you as to the correct style and wording and will show you specimens from which to choose.

> All invitations are sent out about a month beforehand by the bride's people.

All invitations are sent out by the bride's people, the bridegroom supplying a list of those whom he wishes to be asked.

The bride's family are responsible for all the arrangements and expenses in connection with the decoration of the church, the music and form of the service and the reception afterwards.

The bridegroom should make all the necessary arrangements for the publishing of the banns, interviewing the clergy at the church and paying the fees for the actual wedding service.

Soon after the invitations are sent out, wedding presents will start to come in - an invitation to a wedding demands a present, you know, whether the person invited accepts or declines.

The bride or bridegroom should acknowledge all presents received, with the names of the donors. This will come in handy if a report of the wedding is wanted by the local paper, and prevents confusion when the presents are put on view at the reception. The cards which accompany presents should be kept with them, too, so that they can be displayed at the same time.

The arrangements for the wedding should be such as to be well within the means of the bride's parents. It is quite unnecessary to have an elaborate wedding if this will mean a strain upon the family resources. If liked, only the nearest relations and friends can be asked, or the reception can be dispensed with altogether.

A Wedding on Simple Lines

A "white wedding" is, of course, charming, but the bride who has to consider money matters carefully will probably find that a simple frock or costume is much more practical than white satin for which she will have very little use afterwards. She can then dispense with bridesmaids - or have just one attendant, and everything can be run on much simpler and more economical lines.

Suppose, however, that a wedding in the full traditional style is decided upon, here are some of the points that will have to be dealt with.

Bridesmaids

A bride can have as many (within reason) or as few bridesmaids as she likes. Bridesmaids should always be unmarried, and it is usual to ask one or more of her sisters if she has any, and a sister or near relative of the bridegroom, if possible. She can also ask any of her own particular girl-friends, or any small children she may know, to be train-bearers.

When the question of bridesmaids has been settled, the bride has the privilege of deciding what they shall wear. But, while the decision rests with her, she should remember to consult their taste as far as possible, and as they are expected to pay for their own outfits, she should not run them into greater expense than they can afford.

Presents

It is custom for the bridegroom to give each of the bridesmaids a present, either jewellery, or a handbag - generally something is chosen that can be worn at the wedding, though this isn't essential. These presents are dispatched to the bridesmaids shortly before the wedding, or handed to them personally.

The bride and bridegroom also give each other a present, either jewellery, or some article for personal use, and these are generally displayed with the other presents at the reception. (If the bride receives jewellery, she may, of course, prefer to wear it at the wedding.)

The Best Man

The bridegroom asks a brother or one of his bachelor friends to be his best man. The best man is expected to bear any expenses connected with his own travelling, hotel, etc., it is not necessary for the bridegroom to offer to defray these.

The Usher

At most weddings, one or two men friends of bride and bridegroom act as ushers at the church. The ideal is to have equal numbers of the bride's and bridegroom's friends.

Those who are best acquainted with the bride's friends can then show them to their places, and the bridegroom's ushers can show his folk to their seats on the other side of the church. The number of ushers varies according to the size of the wedding.

The Reception

The reception can take place either at the bride's house, or at an hotel or hired rooms.

Sometimes, if the bride's people do not live in a very large house, a relation may lend their house for the occasion.

The catering can be done by the bride's mother, but it is generally more convenient to put this into the hands of professional caterers, who will supply an estimate to suit the amount you wish to spend.

Caterers will, if required, supply everything that is needed; tables, chairs, napery, cutlery, glass and silver, wedding cake and wines, besides the eatables.

Bouquets and Cars

The bridegroom pays for the bridesmaids' and bride's bouquets.

The bride's father pays for that of his wife.

The bridegroom arranges for the car or taxi which is to take himself and his best man to the church.

The bride's father pays for the cars which will transport the bridal party to the church.

The guests make their own arrangements as to conveyances.

On the Day

When the great day arrives, the bride should start to array herself in her wedding finery in good time. If she wishes it, the dressmaker or shop from which she bought her dress will send one of her assistants to help her put on her frock and adjust her veil. Very often it is found convenient for the bridesmaids to change at the bride's house, and the chief bridesmaid should be ready in time to help.

The mother of the bride should be the first to start for the church. The bridesmaids follow next, and they should be at the church for a few minutes before the bride is due to arrive. The bride and her father are the last to arrive.

It is the bride's privilege to be a few minutes late if she likes - but it should not be more than a few minutes, out of consideration for the guests and the clergy - and the poor bridegroom!

The bride and bridegroom should not see each other on the day of the wedding until they meet at the church; it is considered very unlucky! Etiquette demands that the bridegroom shall not spend the night under the same roof as his bride the night before the wedding. If the wedding is held at some distance from his home he must stay with friends or put up at an hotel.

At the Church

The bridegroom must be at the church before the time the service is due to begin. He arrives, accompanied by his best man, at least ten minutes or longer before the scheduled time, and takes up his place in the front pew on the right-hand side of the church, next to the aisle.

The bride's mother sits in the front pew on the left side of the aisle, with any of the bride's near relations. All other seats on the left side of the church are reserved for the bride's friends and relations - those on the right, for the bridegroom's. The father and mother and near relations of the bridegroom have the pew immediately behind the bridegroom and best man.

The Procession

When the bride and her father arrive at the church, they will find the bridesmaids waiting in the porch, with the ushers ready to receive them. The procession lines up in the order previously arranged. If there are any small children among the bride's attendants they should walk immediately behind the bride, holding up her train if she has one.

The organist, who should be given the signal by one of the ushers, now strikes up the voluntary or hymn and the bridal procession moves up the church, the bride on her father's right arm.

As the procession arrives opposite the pew, the bridegroom moves out and stands on the bride's right, with the best man just behind him and a little to his right.

The Wedding Ring

When the time comes, the best man produces the ring, which he hands to the bridegroom. This, of course, has been bought beforehand by the bridegroom, and tried on the bride's finger, but it is the best man's responsibility to see that it is ready to hand when wanted. The chief bridesmaid should be ready to take the bride's bouquet and gloves at the right moment.

The Ceremony

As the bride and bridegroom move forward to the altar steps, the bridesmaids and pages remain standing in the aisle, the best man steps back to his pew, and the bride's father joins his wife.

When the ceremony is over, the newly-married pair proceed into the vestry to sign the register, followed by the bridesmaids, the best man and the families of both bride and bridegroom. None but near relations go into the vestry.

When the register has been signed, the bridegroom offers his right arm to the bride and they walk down the aisle to the strains of the wedding march, followed by the bridesmaids.

The couple get into the waiting car, which is the first to leave the church.

The bridesmaids and the parents of the couple come next, and then the guests make their own way to the reception place.

The Reception

The bride's mother receives the guests as they arrive at the reception. The bride's father should be close at hand, and the bridal couple stand quite near to the hostess, so that guests pass on to them next. The bridesmaids are generally grouped together somewhere near to the bride.

Once the guests havel been received, refreshments are served. The best method is for the guests to stand about or sit at small tables, and the refreshments are handed round by the servants or waiters, who also take round the champagne, ready poured out and the glasses placed on trays.

Cutting the Cake

The bride cuts the cake, which generally stands in the centre of the buffet table from which the refreshments are served. If her husband is a soldier, it is customary for her to use his sword. In any case, she need only cut the first slice.

When the guests have finished eating, they generally wander about, chatting to each other, and go and inspect the presents, which are arranged in a separate room.
It is always as well to have some responsible person in charge of these, as unauthorised persons have been known to find their way into wedding receptions with an eye to the valuables which they know they will find displayed there!

Proposing the Toast

Nowadays speeches are usually dispensed with - except one short speech proposing the bride's health. Some male relative is generally asked to undertake this - not the bride's father. The bridegroom replies for himself and his wife.

Arrangements should be made for the chauffeurs of guests to be given refreshments either in the kitchen, or in some room set apart for them, and someone should be told to see that they have all that they require.

Going Away

In good time to catch their train - or, if they are going away by car, after an hour's time - the bride and bridegroom slip away to change into their going away clothes. The chief bridesmaid accompanies the bride, and helps her off with her things, and sees that her suit-case is packed with all that she will require. The best man performs the same duties for the bridegroom.

A Shower of Rice and Confetti

When the couple come downstairs, the guests gather round to speed them off, and they will be lucky if they escape a shower of rice and confetti and the traditional old shoe attached to their car! If they are going away by train, the best man and the bridesmaids and some of the nearer relations sometimes follow them to the station.

The best man should make it his business to see that a carriage has been reserved on the train, that the newly-wed husband has the tickets, passports, etc., and enough money!

He should tip the porters, and generally make things as easy as possible for them.

Photographs

If photographs of the wedding group are wanted, a photographer should be engaged beforehand, and he will attend at the reception, and pose the party in the part of the house or garden most suitable.

A Report in the Newspaper

When a report of the wedding is asked for by the local newspaper, an account of the dresses worn by the bride, bridesmaids, bride's and bridegroom's mothers, a list of the presents, and the guests who have "accepted" should be written out ready and sent in to the paper beforehand.

Should a reporter turn up at the wedding reception, one of the bridesmaids is usually told to give him any information he may require.

The guests take their departure as soon as the bridal couple have left.

TITLES - WRITTEN AND SPOKEN

Engaged!

– and to the one man in all the world she really wanted!

It had been love at first sight with her, but he just couldn't seem to "see" her at all, until she had read an advertisement just like the one you are now reading, which told her she could win the man she loved by simply understanding certain little peculiarities of man's psychology.

She sent for "Fascinating Womanhood," that amazing new book that shows how you can apply these simple principles of human nature. You, too, can attract and win the man of your choice with the help of this wonderful book.

Write your name and address on the margin of this advertisement, and send it to us with two 1½d. stamps. We will then send you, without the slightest obligation, our new 24-page booklet describing "Fascinating Womanhood." You will enjoy it better than anything you have ever read, but to make sure of your copy you should post your application NOW to:

THE PSYCHOLOGY PRESS

32, Victoria Street, London, S.W.1

H.N.S.S.

TITLES - WRITTEN AND SPOKEN

There are two distinct sets of rules for addressing titled people - one for the written, one for the spoken form.

Let us take the written form first.

Suppose you have to write to someone who holds a title, the first thing you will want to know is how to address the envelope correctly. The following table will show at a glance which is the correct form to adopt.

Addressing the Envelope ~ a few helpful hints

FOR A FORMAL OR BUSINESS LETTER

Duke or Duchess
His Grace, The Duke of Blankbury
Her Grace, The Duchess of Blankbury

Marquis and Marchioness
The Most. Hon. The Marquis of Blankstone
The Most Hon. The Marchioness of Blankstone

Earl and Countess
The Right Hon. The Earl of Blankley
The Right Hon. The Countess of Blankley

FOR A FRIENDLY LETTER

Duke or Duchess
The Duke of Blankbury
The Duchess of Blankbury

Marquis and Marchioness
The Marquis of Blankstone
The Marchioness of Blankstone

Earl and Countess
The Earl of Blankley
The Countess of Blankley

Addressing the Envelope ~ a few helpful hints

FOR A FORMAL OR BUSINESS LETTER

Baron and Baroness
The Right Hon.
The Lord Blankborough
The Right Hon.
The Lady Blankborough

Baronet and wife
Sir Anthony Blankshire, Bart.
Lady Blankshire

Knight and wife
Sir Charles Blank
Lady Blank

FOR A FRIENDLY LETTER

Baron and Baroness
The Lord Blankborough
The Lady Blankborough

Baronet and wife
Sir Anthony Blankshire, Bart.
Lady Blankshire

Knight and wife
Sir Charles Blank
Lady Blank

How to Begin a Formal or Business Letter

Duke.................... ....My Lord Duke
Duchess...Madam
Marquis...My Lord Marquis
Marchioness ....Madam
Earl, Viscount or Baron ....My Lord
Countess, Viscountess or Baroness...................Madam

How to Close a Formal or Business Letter

Your Grace's most obedient servant
I have the honour to be, my Lord Marquis, your most obedient servant ...
I have the honour to be, your Ladyship's most obedient servant ...
I have the honour to be, your Lordship's/ Ladyship's most obedient servant ...

Note - In formal letters, as above, avoid using the direct you and your. In the case of a Duke and Duchess, substitute "if your Grace will allow me ..." "for your Grace's attention ..." In all other cases, substitute "Your Lordship," or "Your Ladyship."

Baronet and Knight
Sir Ordinary formal business ending
Wife of Baronet and Knight
Madam ditto

How to Begin a Social or Friendly Letter

Duke
Dear Duke of Blankbury/Dear Duke/My dear Duke
Duchess
Dear Duchess of Blankbury/Dear Duchess/My dear Duchess
(According to degree of intimacy)

Marquis, Earl, Viscount or Baron
Dear Lord Blankleigh/My dear Lord Blankleigh
Marchioness, Countess, Viscountess or Baroness
Dear Lady Blankleigh/My dear Lady Blankleigh

Baronet or Knight
Dear Sir John
Wife of Baronet or Knight
Dear Lady Robinson

In all friendly or social letters, finish off according to the rules for ordinary social correspondence.

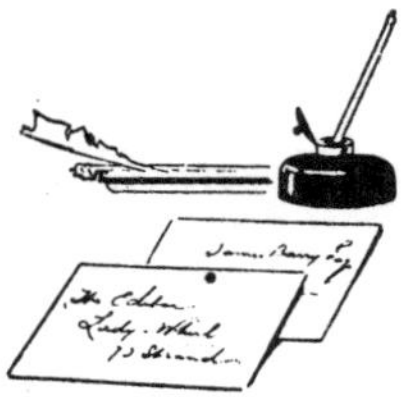

LUCKY BIRTH STONE RING

No. 1	Garnet	for Jan.
„ 2	Amethyst	„ Feb.
„ 3	Blood	„ Mar.
„ 4	Sapphire	„ Apl.
„ 5	Emerald	„ May
„ 6	Agate	„ June
„ 7	Ruby	„ July
„ 8	Diamond	„ Aug.
„ 9	Chrysolite	„ Sep.
„ 10	Opal	„ Oct.
„ 11	Topaz	„ Nov.
„ 12	Turquoise	„ Dec.

WEAR ONE AND BE LUCKY

1/6 POST FREE

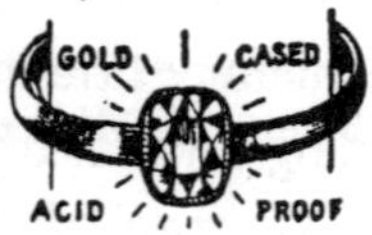

High-grade Lady's or Gent's Ring, with **your own Lucky Stone,** perfect in cut, colour and brilliance. Keeps its colour, guaranteed 5 years. **Adjustable to fit any size finger.** Wonderful Bargain, just to introduce our list. Sent by return with relative Luck-Legend. Luck brings success in competitions and in life generally. **Wear** your Birth-Stone Ring and **BE LUCKY.** State birth-month number for Stone required. **Price 1/6** and **3d.** for Plush-lined Presentation Case to protect Ring in post.

Send NOW 1/9 P.O. to:

Wm. Penn & Co. (DEPT. 12),

682, HOLLOWAY ROAD, LONDON, N.19.

Money Back if not Delighted.

The Services

Officers in the army and navy should have their rank preceding their names on all envelopes. Their titles can be abbreviated here if liked, but not in the actual letter, and remember that "Lieut.-Col. March" is "Dear Colonel March" when you begin your letter.

Never address anyone below the rank of a Captain by his military title in social correspondence. Those holding a naval officer's rank have the letters "R.N." written after their surnames when addressing letters to them, to distinguish them from officers in the army, thus: Captain T.H. Kettle, R.N. The letters "R.N." are not written after an Admiral's name, however.

The Professions

When addressing letters to members of any of the professions, it is correct to include any titles to which they can lay claim.

Doctors generally prefer to be addressed as:

Thomas Dolittle, Esq., M.D.,

but it is not incorrect to address your envelope:

Dr. Thomas Dolittle.

Specialists and surgeons nearly always prefer the

"Esq.," with any appropriate letters after it.

Doctors in other branches of learning are usually addressed with the word "Dr." in front of their name. If they hold a University chair, they may be addressed as "Professor Wiseman". Fellows of the Royal Society should have the initials "F.R.S." after their surname and their other degrees can be added or not, according to taste.

Write the letters "B.A." "B.Sc.," etc, after the "Esq." for holders of ordinary degrees.

Royalty

Letters are never addressed to Royalty, except by their intimate friends. All communications should be sent through one or other of the Court officials.

On being presented to Royalty ladies should curtsey and men should bow.

In conversing with Royalty, the Queen and Princesses are addressed as "Ma'am" (pronounced to rhyme with "jam"!) and the King and any of the Princes as "Sir."

It is not considered correct etiquette to address questions to Royal personages, but where this is absolutely necessary, the words "Your Majesty" should be introduced in the case of the King and Queen.

Should you wish, when in the presence of Royalty, to refer to some other member of the Royal family, don't speak of "The King," or "The Prince of Wales," but instead use the words: "His Majesty," "His Royal Highness," etc.

Remember that any Royal invitation is really a "command" and cannot be refused unless in a case of illness, absence abroad, or some other absolutely unavoidable cause.

Presentation at Court

Should you wish to be presented at Court, it is necessary to approach a relation or some woman whom you know well who has herself been presented, and ask her if she is willing to present you. If she agrees, she will make the necessary application to the Lord Chamberlain.

A woman, who has been presented, can, of course, present her own daughter.

OFFICE ETIQUETTE

Too much make-up, over-polished nails or overpowering scent are to be strictly avoided; you don't want to be thought frivolous and flighty if you want to get that job!

OFFICE ETIQUETTE

When you go for an interview with a prospective employer, you want to create the best possible impression; that goes without saying.

Your Appearance

Be sure that your appearance is above reproach, but aim at absolute neatness rather than at ultra smart or fussy clothes.

Shoes, stockings, gloves and handbag ought to be as perfect as possible. Too much make-up, over-polished nails or overpowering scent are to be strictly avoided; you don't want to be thought frivolous and flighty if you want to get that job!

When you Arrive

If you have visiting cards printed, hand one to the clerk or secretary who receives you.

Be sure that you are on the tick of time for your appointment - better a few minutes before time than even a little late.

Be polite, of course, but don't put on any airs and graces for the occasion. Speak quietly but audibly and to the point.

The Interview

Leave it to your interviewer to ask the questions, though if, at the end of your interview, there are any points about which you are not clear, it is in order for you to ask one or two questions.
Don't be too eager in your enquiries about holidays and time off, as this is apt to give the impression that you are not a keen worker. Ask for the terms of your engagement to be sent you in writing, and when you receive the letter, reply to it at once, repeating the terms enumerated.

Punctuality

Try to be very punctual over times of arrival, lunch hour, and so on, and don't get slack about this as time wears on. And don't watch the clock as the time to go home approaches and rush to put on your hat the moment the hour strikes, regardless of whether you have finished your day's work, or whether any of your colleagues are still struggling with a heavy batch of work. The clock watcher seldom gets promotion when the time comes, and the girl who never offers to lend a hand when there is a rush at six o'clock will find she "gets left in the lurch" when her turn comes to work late.

Adapt

If you want to be popular at your new office, adapt yourself to the ways of the others.

The new-comer who is constantly extolling the superior methods she has been used to in her last job is apt to be irritating to the older hands. If you really have some improvement in the office routine to suggest, wait for a few days at least, and then do it with the utmost tact.

Never be too proud to do any job. If you are asked to make the office tea, see that it is a good cup of tea! Do everything as well as possible, and you'll soon be promoted to something better.

Learn All you Can

Keep your eyes and ears open and learn all you can, not only your routine work, but all that goes on in the office. Only in this way can you become useful enough to your employer for he or she to promote you to a more responsible position.

Don't be always asking questions. Of course, while you are new at the work, you must ask for information, but try to find out all you can for yourself. If you want an address, look it up in the files, instead of sitting helplessly while one of the others does it for you.

Your Appearance in the Office ~ a few helpful hints

Always be neat and tidy in your appearance

Avoid anything flashy and conspicuous in the way of clothes.

In slick tailored things you'll look and feel twice as efficient. After all, you wouldn't play tennis in a dance frock, nor go to a ball in your bathing kit, so why go to the office in flowered ninon or a sleeveless dress that would be more at home on the beach or the river?

Don't be always fidgeting with your hair or making up your face in the office. It looks bad and will get you a reputation for frivolousness and slackness which you may not deserve.

Powder your nose and comb your hair in the cloak-room before you start work, and titivate again at lunch time, and then your complexion will stay put till it is time to go home.

HAWKE

Copper Beech Gift Books
www.copperbeechpublishing.co.uk